STEERING

YOUR SHIP

CALLED LIFE

STEERING

YOUR SHIP

CALLED LIFE

Published in Canada by:

Dr. G. A. Lamarche,

186 Algonquin East

Timmins, Ontario.

P4N 1A9

Tel. (705) 264-1555

Fax (705) 268-5034

Library of Congress Cataloging in
Publication Data

Lamarche, Gilles A. 1955 –

STEERING YOUR SHIP CALLED LIFE

ISBN 0-9684945-0-1
1. Personal Achievement   2. Life Skills 3. Mission

Typesetting & Cover Design:
Diana Rorke

Printed in Canada by: Bowne de Montréal

QUOTES:
> Every effort has been made to ensure that
> each author has been properly acknowledged,
> although some sources were not traceable.
>
> All quotes utilized are part of the thousands
> that the author has accumulated during his
> personal and professional development.

To my children,
Alanna, Christopher and Jason,
who give me joy

To my sweetheart, Renée,
who gives me strength

To my parents,
who taught me to give

To my patients,
who give me courage

To my teachers,
who taught me perseverance

ACKNOWLEDGEMENTS

Many people give their precious time whenever I ask for help. Their honesty and insight have allowed me to grow as a person and a doctor.

To all those colleagues, friends, and family, who support and believe in me, thank you.

To members of my office team, who over the years, have always been supportive of all my endeavours; to Janet, Lynn, and Rose, my present support team, you all make my love of sharing and working possible.

To my mentors Dr. James W. Parker and Dr. Mark Victor Hansen, and to all of you across the continent who I am privileged to call friends, you give me vision for the future and encourage my sharing.

Thank you to all the great authors that have allowed me to learn: Jack Canfield, Mark Victor Hansen, Dr. Wayne Dyer, Anthony Robbins, Dr. John Demartini, Rev. Robert Schuller, Dr. Deepak Chopra, Ed Foreman, Zig Zigglar, Napoleon Hill, Dr. Norman Vincent Peale, Louise Hay and countless others.

DEDICATION

This book is dedicated to all who want to fully experience life, to all who have fallen and have had the courage to rise again. It is also dedicated to the memory of my friend and uncle Guy, who lived by the example of this poem:

DON'T QUIT!

WHEN THINGS GO WRONG, AS THEY SOMETIMES WILL,
WHEN THE ROAD YOU'RE TRUDGING SEEMS ALL UPHILL,
WHEN THE FUNDS ARE LOW, AND THE DEBTS ARE HIGH,
AND YOU WANT TO SMILE, BUT YOU HAVE TO SIGH,
WHEN CARE IS PRESSING YOU DOWN A BIT,
REST IF YOU MUST, BUT DON'T YOU QUIT.

LIFE IS QUEER WITH ITS TWISTS AND TURNS,
AS EVERY ONE OF US SOMETIMES LEARNS,
AND MANY A FAILURE TURNS ABOUT
WHEN HE MIGHT HAVE WON HAD HE STUCK IT OUT,
DON'T GIVE UP THOUGH THE PACE SEEMS SLOW,
YOU MAY SUCCEED WITH ANOTHER BLOW.

OFTEN THE GOAL IS NEARER THAN
IT SEEMS TO A FAINT AND FALTERING MAN,
OFTEN THE STRUGGLER HAS GIVEN UP
WHEN HE MIGHT HAVE CAPTURED THE VICTOR'S CUP,
AND HE LEARNED TOO LATE WHEN THE NIGHT SLIPPED DOWN,
HOW CLOSE HE WAS TO THE GOLDEN CROWN.

SUCCESS IS FAILURE TURNED INSIDE OUT,
THE SILVER TINT OF THE CLOUDS OF DOUBT,
AND YOU NEVER CAN TELL HOW CLOSE YOU ARE,
IT MAY BE NEAR WHEN IT SEEMS AFAR,
SO STICK TO THE FIGHT WHEN YOU'RE HARDEST HIT,
IT'S WHEN THINGS SEEM WORST THAT YOU MUSTN'T QUIT!!!

REST IF YOU MUST, BUT DON'T YOU QUIT!

CONTENTS

LIFE

EXPERIENCE SELECTED BY

THE ETERNAL SOUL

A MOTION PICTURE FOR GOD

A CLASSROOM

IN TIME AND SPACE

LEARNING

PLEASURE

TEACHING

SELF DISCOVERY

FAITH

TO MOVE FORWARD
   WITHOUT FEAR

TO PROGRESS

TO LEARN

TO TRUST

TO FEEL SECURE WHEN RELYING
   UPON ANOTHER

A QUALITY OF HUMAN AWARENESS
   UNIQUE IN ALL THE UNIVERSE.

BE HERE

Opportunities to learn are rare.

Opportunities to truly learn
important new information remain
life's most significant moments.

When confronted with such
an opportunity, set aside
other habits of priority.

Focus every cell and fibre
of your being to BE ALIVE.

Alive to receive the learning.

Alive to KNOW.

Free of wondering thoughts.

Master the possibilities
of bold new frontiers.

Overcome all resistance.

Apply qualities of Faith
and Self-Love in every effort
... and Grow.

BE HERE NOW.

SECTION
1

GETTING
FOCUSED

"Whatever you can do,
or dream you can ...
Begin it.

Boldness has Genius,
Power and Magic
in it."

Goethe

"WHAT A FANTASTIC TIME TO BE ALIVE"

Does this hold true for you, or are you more likely to say, *"most of the time I don't have much fun, and the rest of the time I don't have any fun at all".*

Woody Allen

Incredibly talented people are prevented from fully participating in this game called life due to fear, lack of confidence or simply lack of action.

This book is dedicated to raising your self-esteem and your confidence. Its purpose is to inspire you to attain success that perhaps until now, you had only imagined. Its mission is to give you the insight and tools to create this perfect life, so that no matter what obstacles, you have the ability to surmount them. Through your work you shall seek answers to some of life's most important questions:

Why am I here?

What do I have to contribute that will make a difference?

What do I value and truly believe in ?

What is my mission?

Confident self actualizing people have a sense of purpose. They believe that they are important and that they matter. The confident individual understands that attitude originates within, and in itself is of paramount importance. Be aware of what you are good at, seek your special gifts and abilities. Success and satisfaction are simply rewards for contributing your special gifts to those who cross your path, making a difference.

Yes, such endeavours require commitment. Be willing to commit to what you truly value and believe in. Invest time in developing new strategies for your life. Each part of you, spiritual, physical, mental, and emotional must be aligned to win the game of life. The payoff for your commitment will be the accomplishment of your "burning desire", leading you to a level greater than motivation, called inspiration. Yes inspiration. Move forward with purpose and enthusiasm. Be willing to grow daily. Come to life with purpose and passion. Don't let the future be that time when you would wish that you had done what you are not doing now.

Dr. Gilles A. Lamarche

December, 1997.

"ALL THINGS ARE POSSIBLE FOR ME"

Dr. Wayne Dyer

Soren Kirkegaard remarked:

"Life can only be understood backwards;
but it must be lived forwards."

Why do masters continue to practice and seek improvement continuously? They understand that life is about growth, about acquiring and perfecting the skills and knowledge that allow them to say: *"You know what, I think I'm getting better."*

Make your life a never ending education – be adventurous, lead your own journey of discovery, understand that there are no limits.

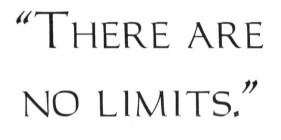

"THERE ARE
NO LIMITS."

Dr. Wayne Dyer

"FAILURE IS,
IN A SENSE,
THE HIGHWAY
TO SUCCESS,
IN AS MUCH AS
EVERY DISCOVERY
OF WHAT IS FALSE,
LEADS US TO SEEK
EARNESTLY AFTER
WHAT IS TRUE."

John Keats

Overcome your weaknesses by leaving them behind. Understand that there is an invisible yet knowable life force within every one of us making all things possible.

"I CONTROL MY THOUGHTS -

THEY ORIGINATE WITHIN ME."

Dr. Wayne Dyer

In his book, <u>Man's Search for Man</u>, Victor Frankl writes:

"Everything can be taken from a man but one thing; the last of human freedoms, to choose one's attitude in any given set of circumstances, to choose one's own way."

Yes, you may be within a particular life crisis at this moment, or you may have experienced a crisis that has left you emotionally or psychologically challenged. Recognize that a crisis is usually nothing more than life's wake up call ... your time to recognize *"all things are possible for me."*

You must be willing to be responsible, to accept responsibility not only for what and who you are, but also for what you can be. The past holds only memories, the future possibilities. I believe that you are never given a thought without also being given the ability to make it come true. Accomplishment requires courage and commitment; it requires that you be willing to plan and act out your burning desire.

Raised in doubt and negativity many of us have been and continue to be our worst enemies. Since all things are possible to he who believes, take time to listen to your little inner voice of limiting beliefs, and replace your beliefs with proactive and self-actualizing thought patterns. Do you recognize some of these statements:

You're not smart enough.
Who do you think you are?
You can't do that.
You dummy.
It will never work.

Take some time now to appreciate the difference between reactive language and proactive language. Read the lines below and make the attempt to honestly position yourself where you think you have been for the last many months or possibly many years.

Understand now, how easy it is to behave towards yourself and others in a proactive fashion, always using proactive language. Sit back and truly appreciate the positive difference of speaking proactive words, and promise yourself that you will be careful to use proactive rather than reactive language when speaking to yourself and others.

REACTIVE LANGUAGE	PROACTIVE LANGUAGE
There's nothing I can do.	*Let's look at our alternatives.*
That's just the way I am.	*I can choose a different approach.*
He makes me so mad.	*I control my own feelings.*
They won't allow that.	*I can create an effective presentation.*
I have to do that.	*I will choose an appropriate response.*
I can't.	*I choose.*
I must.	*I prefer.*
If only.	*I will.*

Take time right now, not tomorrow, now, to identify some of your own limiting thoughts.

_____

_____

_____

_____

_____

_____

_____

_____

_____

_____

_____

_____

_____

_____

_____

_____

_____

_____

_____

_____

_____

THE WILL TO WIN
IS NOT NEARLY
AS IMPORTANT
AS THE WILL
TO PREPARE
TO WIN.

"WE CANNOT BECOME
WHAT WE NEED TO BE,
BY REMAINING
WHAT WE ARE."

Max DePree

The following exercise may allow you to see how limiting we really are to ourselves. Follow the instructions knowing that there is a logical answer which simply may be outside your limiting beliefs.

DIRECTIONS: Without lifting your pencil once started, draw a line that will intersect each and every point in the sequence of nine dots below. The line can change directions once started, but you must not lift your pencil from the page. If you do not succeed after a few attempts consider the fact that there are no limits, draw a sequence of nine dots and try a few more times. Clue: It takes four straight lines connected together to accomplish this task.

●   ●   ●

●   ●   ●

●   ●   ●

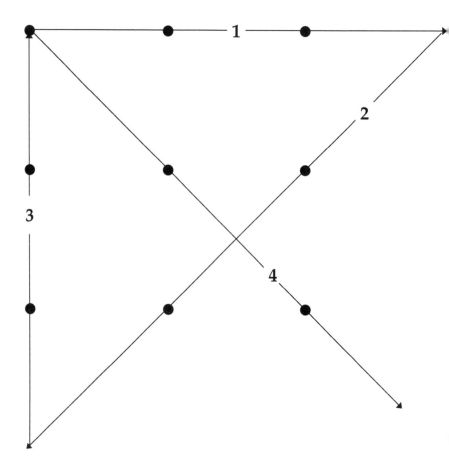

"YOUR MOST

POWERFUL WEAPON

AGAINST LIMITING

THOUGHTS

IS YOUR WILLINGNESS

TO CLARIFY AND ENVISION

WHAT YOU TRULY WANT

FOR YOUR LIFE."

David MacNally

When entertaining the answer to this puzzle, did you actually think beyond the perimeter? Never assume a mental perimeter around any problem. Often solutions lie on the outside. Limiting thoughts are painful realizations; unlimited thoughts, welcome partners in a life of fulfillment. Begin now and persist in stimulating your imagination with the most powerful pictures of what your future holds for you. Visualizing is realizing. (See Section III of this book)

Winners make

commitments,

losers make alibis.

Be a winner.

Commit to Action.

Now think with your mind and feel with your heart, and write down at least five burning desires you want to have happen in your life.

1. _____

   _____

2. _____

   _____

3. _____

   _____

4. _____

   _____

5. _____

   _____

If you truly believe that what you have written are in fact burning desires, conditions, beliefs or circumstances that you wish to see before you as a reality, write an affirmation that describes each situation as real, use the present as if it had already happened.

AFFIRMATIONS

1. _____
   _____
   _____

2. _____
   _____
   _____

3. _____
   _____
   _____

4. _____
   _____
   _____

5. _____
   _____
   _____

If you keep on doing what you have always done, you will keep getting the results you've always gotten. Negative limiting beliefs are negative affirmations that have consistently limited your achievements. Positive affirmations with an action plan will provide a clear vision – the genesis of creation.

Dr. John Demartini has, for many years, used the following affirmation:

"I AM A GENIUS AND I APPLY MY WISDOM"

David McNally, author, entrepreneur, states that the following affirmation has been of significant help in clearing the cobwebs of his own limitations:

"I ACCEPT, I ACKNOWLEDGE

ONLY THOSE THOUGHTS

THAT CONTRIBUTE TO MY SUCCESS."

Two of my favourite affirmations that I recite many times each day are:

"SUCCESS EXISTS FOR ME,

I HAVE THE RIGHT TO IT."

"PATIENTS ARE

MAGNETICALLY ATTRACTED

TO OUR CLINIC."

For many years I have consistently utilized the affirmation which I discovered at the Parker School for Professional Success.

"THROUGH THE INFINITE POWER
OF LIFE WITHIN ME,
I DO WHAT I SHOULD DO
ENTHUSIASTICALLY
AND SUCCESSFULLY.
SUCCESS EXISTS FOR ME,
I HAVE THE RIGHT TO IT,
FOR TO THE BEST OF MY ABILITY
AND KNOWLEDGE
I AM FULFILLING MY DESTINY
HERE ON EARTH.
I EXPRESS LIFE, THE GOOD LIFE,
IN A FULL AND WHOLESOME WAY,
AND I GREET EACH NEW DAY
WITH COURAGE AND
UNDERSTANDING."

This affirmation has often allowed me to face up to situations which I found truly difficult. In honesty, reciting this affirmation has had such an impact on my life that I may not be here today had it not been for these transforming words.

YOUR DESTINY IS DETERMINED BY CHOICE NOT CHANCE.

"THE MIND, ONCE EXPANDED,

NEVER RETURNS

TO ITS FORMER SIZE,

LIMITATION OR SHAPE."

Dr. B. J. Palmer

"A MAN OF HUMANITY

IS ONE WHO ...

DESIRING ATTAINMENT

FOR HIMSELF,

HELPS OTHERS TO ATTAIN."

Confucius

Understand that in this century or others that have preceded, singleness of purpose with vision, action and desire have allowed people to succeed.

People care not how much you know until they know how much you care, no matter what your profession or business.

Create your vision with the thought of others in mind. Quietly, in your own mind and heart, say *"I Am Confident"* and go on.

BEFORE THE ART OF YOUR PROFESSION, COMES THE ART OF BELIEF.

Success is

a resolution

that is

not afraid

of sacrifice.

"SUCCESSFUL COUNTRIES
AND INDIVIDUALS SUCCEED
BECAUSE THEY HAVE A DREAM,
A VISION, A FUTURE.
BUT IN ORDER FOR THEIR DREAMS
OR VISIONS TO BE SUCCESSFUL
OR ATTAINABLE
THEY MUST TAKE ACTION.
VISION WITHOUT ACTION
IS MERELY A DREAM.
ACTION WITHOUT VISION
JUST PASSES TIME.
VISION WITH ACTION
CAN CHANGE THE WORLD."

Joel Arthur Baker

I HAVE NOT FAILED
10,000 TIMES.

I HAVE SUCCESSFULLY FOUND
10,000 WAYS
THAT DON'T WORK.

Thomas A. Edison

SECTION

II

DEFINING

YOUR

MISSION

Clarifying What Matters Most To You

"ALL THINGS ARE DIFFICULT BEFORE THEY ARE EASY."

Mark Twain

WHAT IS YOUR MISSION STATEMENT?

"I hereby pledge my life to my greatest
self expression of love and service,
for the benefit of all humanity."

Gilles A. Lamarche D. C.

ARE YOU PASSIONATE?

PASSIONATE: *"Showing or inspired by*
a strong emotion."

Ask yourself:

> *What message can I communicate clearly*
> *with passion?*

Recognize that:

> *Without passion your message is dead.*
>
> *Without passion you have no mission.*
>
> *Your life will be most fulfilling when pursued*
> *with passion.*

To be nourished, be nourishing. Learn to share your message with the world, whatever it might be, with passion. Get inspired and excited.

Write statements describing your work or profession using your innate senses and practice feeling the words. You can do this.

_____

_____

_____

_____

_____

_____

_____

_____

_____

_____

_____

_____

_____

_____

"Above all to thine own self be true."

In creating your mission statement, you will want to hold the above words very close to your heart. You might ask, how can I be true to myself? Be truthful in defining and describing what you truly want for your life. Assess your understanding of success by considering the following questions and any others you might add:

Whom do I know that is successful?

_____

_____

Why do I regard them as so?

_____

_____

My definition of success is:

_____

_____

The feelings I associate with success are:

_____

_____

What am I willing to do to achieve success?

_____

_____

What am I not willing to do?

_____

_____

You have often heard the statement "Life is a school." I believe this statement, and I also regard life as a game, one that usually gives us what we deserve, because we always get out of life what we put into life. How do we determine the score of this game called life? Part of the winning philosophy is to succeed. But, what really constitutes success? What brings happiness and all the rest?

The greatest ability given us by God is the power of choice. Success and happiness result from the choices we make in our lives. One of those choices might be to do something worthwhile and satisfying, while another would be the action steps we take to achieve our goals.

Success can mean so many different things to as many different people. Perhaps the best way to describe success is:

"TO BE INVOLVED WITH AND ACCOMPLISHING

THAT WHICH RESULTS IN THE FEELINGS

WE WANT TO EXPERIENCE MOST OF THE TIME."

David McNally

When you are a willing and committed participant in the game called life, you are a winner. Success is not measured by what you have but rather who you are. It matters not what you achieve in physical goods but rather who you become in the process of this wonderful experience.

To be a fully functioning human being, you must do what you love, and love what you do, because what you do is an expression of your gifts and talents.

You are captain of your ship called life.

When considering your mission statement, please understand the difference between career and vocation. Career is goal oriented (physical plane), but vocation is purpose oriented (spiritual plane).

When you become passionate about your career, your career becomes your vocation and you can't help reaching the goals you set. Create a mission and purpose greater than yourself. When you seek to be fulfilled in your career, you become committed to doing and being the best. You exceed your own expectations and discover that career goals are more easily achieved when you are working on purpose. There is a purpose for our lives greater and more significant than you might have ever considered.

Henry Thoreau wrote:

"The mass of men lead lives of quiet desperation."

Dr. Wayne Dyer wrote:

"My life has purpose. There are no limits, because I overcome weakness by leaving it behind."

Are you willing to utilize the invisible yet knowable life force within you, or are you satisfied to live in desperation. If you are presently in desperation, realize that this is simply a smoke screen of bigger and better days ahead. The road which follows is that of the stronger man who sooner or later says, *"I can"*.

Always remember that it matters not how many times you fall, only how many times you get up. You exist to contribute, to serve, to reach beyond yourself and make a difference in this wonderful world. Your life is important, what you can contribute is necessary and needed. You matter.

Let your heart do your thinking and let your head begin to feel, you too will see the world anew and know what's truly real.

When mind and heart are in harmony tune into that melody. While goals nourish the heart, purpose feeds the soul. Be committed to a compelling mission.

LIFE

LIFE IS A GIFT - ACCEPT IT

LIFE IS AN ADVENTURE - DARE IT

LIFE IS A MYSTERY - UNFOLD IT

LIFE IS A GAME - PLAY IT

LIFE IS A STRUGGLE - FACE IT

LIFE IS BEAUTY - PRAISE IT

LIFE IS A PUZZLE - SOLVE IT

LIFE IS AN OPPORTUNITY - TAKE IT

LIFE IS SORROWFUL - EXPERIENCE IT

LIFE IS SONG - SING IT

LIFE IS A GOAL - ACHIEVE IT

LIFE IS A MISSION - FULFILL IT

Please sit quietly listening to inspiring music or looking at inspiring scenery. Breathe deeply and allow innate to penetrate your every cell. Allow innate to provide you with your mission and translate it onto paper. Work this statement until you bond so tightly that it becomes you.

"Above all to thine own self be true."

MY MISSION IN LIFE

_____

_____

_____

_____

_____

_____

_____

_____

THE PRIMARY REASON
OR PURPOSE
OF EVERY LIVING
HUMAN BEING:

TO BE OF SERVICE.

How you live your life and what you do with it, shapes not only your future but that of everyone you touch. You are important in the global picture of life; you can affect the lives of so many people.

Each of us has a purpose, and as proactive individuals our purpose is to somehow make a positive contribution to the people in this world we live in. Nothing will have a more positive effect on your level of success, fulfillment and happiness, than the belief and understanding that you bring something special to humanity, something that no one else can offer quite like you. The most important thought that you can ever hold is: *"My life matters, I matter"*. Learn to convey the passion you feel for what you do. Do what you love, love what you do and love those that surround you and those you have not had the privilege to meet.

The Love Concept is worthy of being taught and delivered to every human being on our planet. When you live this fact, your commitment to participate in this global goal allows the phenomenon of meaningful coincidence to take place. This phenomenon simply causes people to show up, the phone to ring, your career or business to blossom.

Life is empty when you are not useful, powerful when on purpose. When we are being useful and loving, happiness, fulfillment, peace and commitment follow. We were all created to fulfil a purpose, chosen to follow this purpose with a burning desire. This purpose will empower and inspire you, and give meaning to your life. Great achievers in this world have had different beliefs, callings, and careers, but each has had the power of purpose to guide their life.

The antithesis of having a purpose is an empty life where there is no meaning, where the daily objective is simply survival. The same holds true for a health care practice. The practice that continually needs to be filled from the outside, requiring constant advertising and gimmicks to attract new patients, is the practice where the doctor and staff lack purpose.

The purpose of life is to be a growing, contributing human being. The purpose of your business and mine, is to serve mankind every moment of every day. Dr. James W. Parker describes those who truly serve as operating on the spiritual level, which attracts patients/clients simply by its existence. No matter what your career or business, this principle holds true for you.

Clearly, what distinguishes truly successful individuals is that they are contributors to the people and the world. They are willing to serve, to give for the sake of giving, providing loving service just to be of service. Their accomplishments, their successes, are rooted in their desire to grow and be of service to all humanity.

If you are to succeed, you must understand that your rewards in life will be in direct proportion to the contribution you make. This is a fundamental principle, apply it to your career and in time you will have little concern over anything on the physical plane, and you will be overwhelmed with love, admiration, and respect.

YOUR REWARDS IN LIFE
ARE IN DIRECT PROPORTION
TO THE CONTRIBUTION
YOU MAKE.

The average individual is in business or working to earn a living. These people are usually desperate and rarely grow beyond the physical/money plane. The real purpose of a career or profession is to create and keep clients by serving. You have a service that everyone needs. By having a service consciousness you too will experience the result and reward of doing things right, and doing the right things. Well serviced and satisfied clients, build profitable and lasting businesses, that function from the inside out.

Accept, right now, where you are and the responsibility for where you want to be. You have the power to affect for better for worse, the present and future state of your career, your relationships, your life.

The world needs leaders that can inspire their fellow colleagues with a fiery sense of mission. Since we all teach what we most need to learn, our bond lies in the common desire to discover a purpose worthy of our deepest commitment. Each night before you go to sleep ask yourself these questions:

Did I today, grow as a Doctor, Lawyer, Teacher...?

Did I today, make the world a better place in which to live?

Did I today, serve for the sake of serving?

Did I today, talk health, and happiness to everyone I met?

Did I today, expect only the best?

Did I today, live according to my mission and purpose in life?

Having purpose is not fantasy for happiness or success. It is however a fundamental answer to what makes life worthwhile.

Nietzsche wrote:

*"He who has a why to life
can bear almost any how."*

The power of purpose will certainly lead you to success. The real treasure lies much more in how it enriches your life. Have the confidence to move forward, to live the life both personally and professionally that you imagined for yourself with sincerity and security. You have the power of purpose, you need only to access its great strength.

"YOUR PAST CANNOT BE CHANGED, BUT YOU CAN CHANGE TOMORROW BY YOUR ACTIONS TODAY."

Since you can change your tomorrow by your actions today, I ask you to take time to become aware of how special you are, by performing the mental gymnastics that follow. Be sincere, use your heart and your head to arrive at your answers. You will be pleasantly surprised.

MY ASSETS ARE:
(qualities and characteristics I regard as valuable)

_____

_____

_____

_____

_____

_____

_____

_____

_____

_____

_____

_____

_____

_____

_____

_____

MY TALENTS ARE:
(abilities and aptitudes)

_____

_____

_____

_____

_____

_____

_____

_____

_____

_____

_____

_____

_____

_____

_____

_____

_____

_____

_____

MY SKILLS ARE:
(competencies acquired through practice)

_____

_____

_____

_____

_____

_____

_____

_____

_____

_____

_____

_____

_____

_____

_____

_____

_____

"Live all you can:

it's a mistake not to.

It doesn't so much matter

what you do in particular,

so long as you live your life.

If you haven't had that,

what have you had?"

Henry James

MY STRENGTHS ARE:
(distinguish the top two from each
of the previous 3 categories)

_____

_____

_____

_____

_____

_____

_____

_____

_____

_____

_____

_____

_____

_____

_____

_____

_____

THE PRINCIPLE OF CONTRIBUTION:
REWARD FOLLOWS SERVICE
GETTING FOLLOWS GIVING
MAKING AN IMPRESSION FOLLOWS
MAKING A DIFFERENCE.

Provide at least three answers to each question below.

Why do I work as a _____?

1. _____

2. _____

3. _____

What does my career mean to me?

1. _____

2. _____

3. _____

What do I expect from my career?

1. _____

2. _____

3. _____

Research has shown three primary reasons why people work:

1. MONEY:
   Basic motivator required to support ourselves and our families.

2. AFFILIATION:
   Feeling connected to others, the need of belonging. Work provides an opportunity for being helpful, goal setting, recognition and support.

3. MEANING:
   When you consistently excel in your work, you receive far greater rewards than money or friendship. Satisfaction and fulfilment increase productivity. People who excel have a sense of purpose, a feeling that their work really matters.

Is there any link between your answers to why you work and the three factors described above? Defining your mission will give greater meaning to why you work, why you do what you do. When your focus is on what you can give, you will be amazed how the other needs are met.

"A MAN IS
A SUCCESS
IF HE GETS UP
IN THE MORNING
AND GETS TO BED
AT NIGHT,
AND IN BETWEEN
DOES WHAT HE
WANTS TO DO."

Bob Dylan

For the majority of us, our work does provide the most significant opportunity to contribute to the world. Gaining a sense of purpose from what we do is therefore the first step in helping us identify our life purpose. Be willing to go out on a limb - that's where the fruit is. Do not suppress or deny your capabilities for the elusion of security. Be willing to step out of your comfort zone and do whatever is necessary to achieve the success that you desire. Please reflect on these questions:

What frame of mind would I like to be in at the onset of each day?

What feeling would I like to experience at the end of each day?

After I have gone, what would I like people to be saying about me?

What do I want my life to stand for?

If I keep on doing what I have been doing, will I get to where I want to be?

Most of us desire the experience of life to be one that we look forward to enjoying every moment of every day. The game of life is meant to be played to the fullest. All active participants win, no matter the score. It is the level of commitment that matters most.

The observers in life watch from the sidelines, stimulated only by the fantasy of playing and suddenly the game is over. Defining your mission implies making a choice to get into the game. The position you play lies in discovering your talents and how best to apply them.

In a Nike television commercial, Michael Jordan states:

"I have made many mistakes; 26 times I have been trusted to make the game winning shot – and missed. I have failed over and over again. That's why I succeed."

This man discovered his talents and continues to understand that it takes practice to improve and you must try and try again in order to succeed.

Consider a time in your life when all was going badly:

How did you think?

What did you do?

What were your feelings?

Now consider a time when you were performing at your best, whether in your career or in another area of your life:

What were your thoughts and feelings then?

How did you behave or react?

What were you doing best?

Please describe a few situations during that time by answering the questions asked above.

1. _____

_____

_____

2. _____

_____

_____

3. _____

_____

_____

4. _____

_____

_____

"IT'S A FUNNY THING ABOUT LIFE,

IF YOU REFUSE TO ACCEPT

ANYTHING BUT THE BEST,

YOU VERY OFTEN GET IT."

W. Sommerset Maugham

Many have offered the adjectives to best describe their worst and best experience as follows:

AT BEST	AT WORST
Confident	Fearful
Enthusiastic	Apathetic
Organized	Messy
Relaxed	Anxious
Focused	No direction
In control	Out of control
Friendly and loving	Argumentative
Decisive	Frustrated

What causes us to consistently perform at our best? People perform at their best when contributing their talents to something they truly believe in. You must find or regain the passion you once had for your career. If the candlelight is only a flicker, meditate and rekindle your passion with purpose.

A great way to restore those feelings of passion and contribution, is to reflect upon, recognize, and be thankful for your assets, strengths, skills and talents. Take time to concentrate, listen to that special little voice inside of you and fill in the page below. Even you will be surprised.

MY ASSETS:

_____

_____

_____

_____

MY SKILLS:

_____

_____

_____

_____

MY TALENTS:

_____

_____

_____

_____

MY STRENGTHS:

_____

_____

_____

_____

The following questions should help you get to the heart of what you truly want for your life. Before writing anything down, reflect on your answers. Connect your thoughts with your feelings and remember that:

"If your heart could do your thinking
and your head began to feel,
you'd see the world anew
and know what's truly real."

This metaphor simply describes that we must think and feel simultaneously to truly change our life.

1. *How would I like to be remembered?*

_____

_____

_____

2. *What have I always dreamed of contributing to the world?*

_____

_____

_____

3. *Looking back on life, what are some of my major contributions?*

_____

_____

_____

4. *When people think of me, what might they say are my most outstanding characteristics?*

_____

_____

_____

5. *What do I really want for my life?*

_____

_____

_____

By working and answering these questions, you are choosing to live with purpose, not by accident, you have decided to live by choice not chance.

By creating your mission or purpose, you are STEERING YOUR SHIP CALLED LIFE. After seriously reflecting on the answers to these questions, put your answers to paper, etch them in concrete if you would.

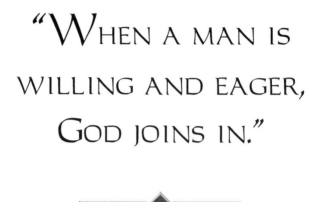

"WHEN A MAN IS WILLING AND EAGER, GOD JOINS IN."

Aeschylus

Now review your answers to those questions; the final exercise is to bring the answers to focus, to define your mission in a statement of purpose that truly expresses your commitment to what you are all about. In preparation consider some of the characteristics of purpose.

A PURPOSE:

- *focuses on Contribution*
- *uses Gifts and Talents*
- *is Meaningful*
- *is Enjoyable*
- *is Continuous*
- *is Inspiring*

There are no limits in time, the clock is not running. Be patient and take all the time you require to truly feel your purpose in the core of your being. This journey of discovery will last a lifetime. As your awareness grows keep your purpose in your mind and in your heart. Keep it close to you in writing so you can review your purpose often until it becomes part of you.

_____

_____

_____

_____

_____

MY MISSION:

I am dedicated to improving
the quality of health care in our world.
I accomplish this by being interested,
loving and caring. I am willing to take a stand
for what I believe in and share openly with humanity.
I accomplish this by sharing information
with patients, colleagues and all I meet.
Innate allows me this travel.

Allow the principle of purpose to work for you. You have gained the knowledge that rewards follow service and you are now free to serve well. By keeping faith and remaining faithful to the principle, you will be astonished by what eventually comes your way, it isn't partial and plays no favourites. People who realize their dreams are not without fear, they are not without butterflies - they simply choose to let their butterflies fly in formation.

Congratulations!
You have arrived.
Welcome!!!

"I OVERCOME WEAKNESS
BY LEAVING IT BEHIND."

Dr. Wayne Dyer

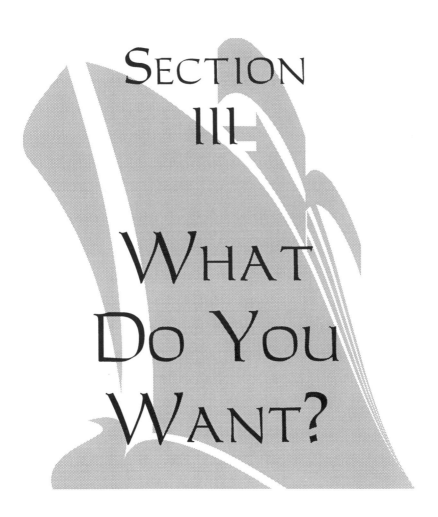

SECTION III

WHAT DO YOU WANT?

CHOICE

YOU CAN CHOOSE
HIGHER CREATIVE ACTIVITY,
SOURCED ONLY IN LOVE.

YOU CAN CHOOSE POSITIVE THINKING
IN YOUR CREATIVE WORK.

YOU CAN CHOOSE TO ACCEPT
ALL THAT YOU CREATE
AND ASSUME RESPONSIBILITY.

ORDERLY ACTION
WILL REPLACE CHAOS.

YOUR FULFILLMENT
WILL ALWAYS FOLLOW.

CHOICE!

THE CHOOSING IS ALWAYS
IN YOUR CONTROL.

CHOOSE NOW.
CHOOSE WELL.

What do you truly want? If you knew you could not fail, what would you choose to be, do or have? Do you realize that you control your thoughts, they originate within you and therefore all things are possible for you?

Most of us lack the awareness that we have considerable influence over the outcome of our life; this becomes a barrier to fulfillment. Successful people plan, design and they work hard and smart to achieve. They understand the following formula:

$$E + R = O$$

EVENT + REACTION = OUTCOME

If you know what outcome you expect or would like to have, your reaction will always be in correlation with that outcome no matter what the event. If you begin your day expecting it to be terrific and accept nothing less, you have chosen your outcome. Never lose sight of the outcome you choose and learn to react to events that occur in your life with the purpose of achieving that outcome.

A second barrier to success is the feeling of being undeserving of fulfilling your dreams. This is due to misinformation which has permeated our being from childhood. The truth of the matter is that as a member of the human race, it is your heritage, your right, to participate in this wonderful game of life at what ever level you desire.

Another common barrier is cultural. Due to the environment and culture in which you are raised, you may have a sense that only certain goals are possible for you. Recognize that no goal is too small or too large if you wish to accomplish it. Also realize that success is not measured by the size of the goal or the accomplishment.

If you can clearly visualize what it is that you want and believe that you have the capacity to achieve it, and if you are willing to invest both time and energy in getting it, then this accomplishment is possible for you. Always, always be true to yourself.

Creating a vision starts with displaying in your own mind and on paper everything you dare to imagine possible for your life. You are given permission to let your imagination go wild and free. Allow every desire, dream, hope, and fantasy to come into your mind and as they arrive write them down. This is your movie and you are the only one watching.

Everything is possible. Always remember that anything great that has ever occurred in this world started as a single thought in one person's mind. If it is possible for that person, then it is also possible for you, because every human being is given the capacity and the capabilities to achieve. Once you have laid out a certain number of your desires, it becomes interesting to activate your mind by utilizing different types of visualization techniques available. Aristotle commented that the soul never thinks without a picture.

Therefore it is imperative that you learn the technique of creative visualization. You are the director of the movies in your mind, and only you can choose the type of imagery that you respond to best.

FIVE DIFFERENT KINDS OF IMAGERY

1. SPONTANEOUS:

   Allowing unbidden images to simply pop into your mind.

2. INDUCED:

   Consciously select an end goal image. Truly imagine what it is that you want to achieve and visualize that particular image.

3. CONCRETE VERSUS ABSTRACT:

   As in visualizing healthy lungs (concrete) or the universal symbol of a red circle with a red bar slashing through a cigarette to represent the stop smoking symbol.

4. GENERAL VERSUS SPECIFIC:

   Visualizing a stack of money versus seeing yourself with $100,000.00.

5. END GOAL:

   Seeing yourself earn $100,000 this year

   VERSUS

   PROCESS:

   Imagery of mentally going from task to task, day after day, until you reach your goal.

Please practice each type of imagery until you find the one or the few that you feel most comfortable with. Like anything new, directing your mind's movies takes some time to master.

Different visualization techniques are useful to achieve different end goals. While visualizing, attempt to combine the left brain focus with your right brain playfulness. Visualization should have the quality of playful focus. For those of us who are more technical in our thinking, more left brain, let loose and make this the game that it should be. Six particular visualization techniques are described below.

1. COLLAGE:

    Create a montage of five or six different mental snapshots of your end goal being achieved. In other words see yourself already there.

2. STROBING or FLASHING:

    Rapidly flash or strobe your end goal picture on and off for thirty seconds to imprint it in your mind.

3. COMPUTER GENERATED:

    Begin with one coloured dot on your mental computer screen. Within thirty seconds, generate thousands of coloured dots to represent your end goal picture.

4. MULTI-FOCUS:

   Project beams of energy or light from your forehead, heart, and solar plexus to create a 3-D picture of your goal where the beams meet and overlap six feet or so in front of you.

5. EXPLOSIVE:

   Picture your old pre-goal self, painted in dull, drab colours, then in two seconds or less explode it away and replace it with your new end goal picture in bright colours.

6. IN/OUT VISUALIZATION:

   Go back and forth inside your body, looking at your end goal picture; then go outside your body and see yourself in the picture as having successfully attained your goal. When performing this exercise allow 15-30 seconds for each sequence.

WHEN AND HOW TO PROGRAM FOR CHANGE

"The human mind is our fundamental resource."

John F. Kennedy

Mental programming is simply educating and re-educating your subconscious, creating new mental software using words, mental pictures, and feelings.

Three basic tools must be present for all change to occur:

1. DESIRE:

    You must want something to change.
    You must have a burning desire and vision.

2. EXPECTATION:

    Knowing and expecting that what you are doing will work with repetition and determination

3. IMAGINATION:

    Creating mental movies of your desired goal and taking the required action steps.

BRAIN WAVE FREQUENCIES

CYCLES/SECOND		
45	BETA	**WAKING STATE** Reasoning, logic Decision-making Consciousness
12	ALPHA	**HYPNOTIC STATE** Common in Meditators Most receptive to new learning
8	THETA	**DREAM STATE** Pre-sleep Reverie State Creativity
4	DELTA	**DEEP SLEEP STATE**

You will notice at 12 cycles per second, the hypnotic state, the mind appears to be most receptive to new learning. Since visualization may be a new form of learning for you, it will be best to practice in the alpha state. You are usually in the alpha state upon awakening in the morning and shortly before going to sleep at night. We therefore suggest that you practice your visualization at least twice per day, morning and night.

"THE INDISPENSABLE
FIRST STEP
TO GETTING
THE THINGS
YOU WANT
OUT OF LIFE
IS TO DECIDE
WHAT YOU WANT."

Bob Stein

SECTION
IV

GOAL
SETTING
STRATEGIES

COURAGE

COURAGE IS
THAT ONE INGREDIENT
WHICH SEPARATES
THE STRONG FROM THE WEAK,
THE SUCCESSFUL
FROM THE UNSUCCESSFUL,
THE GREAT FROM THE AVERAGE.

ALL THE THINGS
YOU DESIRE IN LIFE
HAVE ONE COMMON HANDLE,
WHICH IS MADE FOR THE HAND
OF THE MAN OF

COURAGE.

Reaching a goal is easy; setting one and staying on target may sometimes be difficult. The following few pages are to be used as your goal planner. Read this strategy section before writing anything. Then read the entire planner and fill in page 74 entitled "MY PERSONAL COMMITMENT." Following this, fill out your master goal list on pages 75-76 of this planner. Be bold and write everything you want to be, do, or have, even if it might seem unrealistic at this present time. Be very specific and describe each goal with suitable adjectives. It is better to write down too many than too few goals.

Now go to page 77 and transfer the goals from your master list that you consider to be short range goals, (less than one year). Set a realistic date for each accomplishment. Always remember that no goal is unrealistic; time frames dictate the realism. On the next page transfer your intermediate range goals, (one to three years) and on the page following this transfer your long range goals.

Choose one to four short range goals that you can work on daily and identify these in step one, on page 82. Go through each step on pages 82-83 listing major obstacles, intellectual property required etc. This is necessary to help you identify what you require and what you already possess for the achievement of your goal.

Page 85 requires that you fill in your daily activities towards the achievement of your goals. Follow the directions on that page. You may want to photocopy a number of these pages so that you will have one for each week of the year. Pages 75-76 can also be copied since every important goal is viewed step by step as suggested.

Examine your goals and priorities. Always remember to try and create balance in your life, setting goals in each of the seven categories listed.

Read your goals three times per day, morning, noon, and night. It is preferable to read them out loud. You may want to record yourself on an audio cassette and listen to yourself while driving to and from work.

Take approximately one half hour weekly to review your goals and about two hours per quarter, every thirteen weeks or so, to adjust your goals, strategies, and accomplishments. Remember that every goal achieved is a victory in your file of life. Treat your accomplishments as such and congratulate yourself. Once you have completed this planner for the first time, you will have spent more time goal setting than most people do in an entire life time.

Congratulations

and

Go For It!!!

ACTION WILL ELIMINATE FEAR,

SO STEP INTO ACTION NOW.

IF YOUR GOAL

PENETRATES AND PERMEATES

THE INNER SPACES OF YOUR MIND,

AS A CRYSTAL CLEAR VISUALIZATION

OF YOUR IMAGINATION,

IT WILL INEVITABLY BECOME

YOUR REALIZATION.

MY PERSONAL COMMITMENT

I, _____, *promise that I will take steps forward to accomplish my goals.*

I am willing to say "NO" to the pleasures of the day so that I can say "YES" to the happiness of a LIFETIME.

I realize that attitude, knowledge, time, and desire are investments for a successful life, and I am willing to obtain and cultivate these investments.

I further realize that success is a journey and not a destination and as such already see myself as successful, happy and healthy.

I know that success is the progressive realization of my worthwhile goals and ambitions, and to those ends, I promise to work daily.

Affirmed this ____ day of _____ , _____ , at _____ , _____ .

_____
(signature)

MY GOALS MASTER LIST

My future accomplishments and acquisitions

_____

_____

_____

_____

_____

_____

_____

_____

_____

_____

_____

_____

_____

_____

_____

Goals should then be classified according to their time schedule and possibilities. Set realistic target dates to achieve **Victory**.

SHORT RANGE GOALS
(less than one year)

GOAL   DATE

_____   _____

_____   _____

_____   _____

_____   _____

_____   _____

_____   _____

_____   _____

_____   _____

_____   _____

_____   _____

_____   _____

_____   _____

INTERMEDIATE GOALS
(one to three years)

GOAL	DATE
_____	_____
_____	_____
_____	_____
_____	_____
_____	_____
_____	_____
_____	_____
_____	_____
_____	_____
_____	_____
_____	_____
_____	_____
_____	_____
_____	_____
_____	_____

LONG RANGE GOALS
(three years or more)

GOAL   DATE

_____   _____

_____   _____

_____   _____

_____   _____

_____   _____

_____   _____

_____   _____

_____   _____

_____   _____

_____   _____

_____   _____

_____   _____

"LIVE YOUR LIFE EACH DAY
AS YOU WOULD CLIMB A MOUNTAIN.

AN OCCASIONAL GLANCE
TOWARD THE SUMMIT
KEEPS THE GOAL IN MIND,
BUT MANY BEAUTIFUL SCENES
ARE TO BE OBSERVED
FROM EACH NEW VANTAGE POINT.

CLIMB SLOWLY, STEADILY,
ENJOYING EACH PASSING MOMENT;
AND THE VIEW FROM THE SUMMIT
WILL SERVE AS A FITTING CLIMAX
FOR THE JOURNEY."

Harold V. Melchert

"THE HIGHEST
REWARD
FOR A PERSON'S TOIL
IS NOT WHAT THEY
GET FOR IT,
BUT WHAT THEY
BECOME BY IT."

John Ruskin

GENERAL GOALS
List only goals you can work on daily

STEP #1   GOAL IDENTIFICATION

_____

_____

_____

STEP #2   OBSTACLES IN REACHING THIS GOAL

_____

_____

_____

STEP #3   INTELLECTUAL PROPERTY REQUIRED

_____

_____

_____

STEP #4   HUMAN TALENT REQUIRED

_____

_____

_____

STEP #5 EXPECTED BENEFITS

_____

_____

_____

STEP #6 ACTION PLAN

_____

_____

_____

STEP #7 AFFIRMATION TO SUPPORT GOAL

_____

_____

_____

STEP #8 MENTAL PICTURE

_____

_____

_____

STEP #9 ESTIMATED DATE OF ACHIEVEMENT

_____

_____

_____

"IF A PERSON
ADVANCES CONFIDENTLY
IN THE DIRECTION
OF THEIR DREAM,
AND ENDEAVOURS
TO LIVE THE LIFE
THEY HAVE IMAGINED,
THEY WILL MEET
WITH SUCCESS
UNEXPECTED
IN COMMON HOURS."

Thoreau

DAILY ACTIVITY SHEET

DATE: _____

GOAL	ONE	TWO	THREE	FOUR
MONDAY				
TUESDAY				
WEDNESDAY				
THURSDAY				
FRIDAY				
SATURDAY				
SUNDAY				

N.B. Always remember to set goals that will allow you to achieve balance in your life.

The categories to be considered are:

◊ CAREER

◊ FAMILY

◊ SOCIAL

◊ FINANCIAL

◊ PHYSICAL

◊ MENTAL

   and

◊ SPIRITUAL

In filling in the activity sheet on page 85, write in a large "V" for victory when you achieve a goal. This appears to provide energy for continuing this process.

On a certain day, if you do nothing towards the advancement of a particular goal, write in "NOTHING" in that particular column. That too will stimulate you to take action.

This is easy work ... *Just Do It!*

JUST
DO IT!

"THE MAJORITY OF MEN

MEET WITH FAILURE

BECAUSE OF THEIR

LACK OF PERSISTENCE

IN CREATING NEW PLANS

TO TAKE THE PLACE

OF THOSE WHICH FAIL."

Napoleon Hill

SECTION V

TOOLS OF THE TRADE

Develop Your Communication Skills

I Hear - I Forget

I See - I Remember

I Do - I Understand

Confucius

"A PERSON FIRST STARTS TO LIVE
WHEN HE CAN HAVE AS MUCH REGARD
FOR HIS FELLOW MAN AS HE DOES FOR HIMSELF."

"I BELIEVE WE ARE HERE TO DO GOOD."

"IT IS THE RESPONSIBILITY
OF EVERY HUMAN BEING TO INSPIRE
TO DO SOMETHING WORTHWHILE,
TO MAKE THIS WORLD A BETTER PLACE
THAN THE ONE THAT HE FOUND."

"LIFE IS A GIFT,
AND IF WE AGREE TO ACCEPT IT,
WE MUST CONTRIBUTE IN RETURN.
WHEN WE FAIL TO CONTRIBUTE,
WE FAIL TO ADEQUATELY ANSWER
WHY WE ARE HERE."

Albert Einstein

One of the major reasons why many people fail to contribute, is their inability to properly communicate. The number one fear of adults in North America is considered to be the fear of public speaking. The second fear is said to be the fear of dying. This would appear to mean that most people would rather die than speak in public.

In every profession, it is imperative that you develop your communication skills in order to grow. Communication skills require good speaking habits, as well as good listening habits. Body language also remains an important factor. Many books and audio cassette tapes are available on this subject. I urge you to discover and devour the contents of these learning tools. In this chapter we will touch upon some essential communication skills, that once learned, will allow you to enjoy improved relationships with all you encounter.

These skills can be utilized one on one, and later in front of groups. The quicker you learn to effectively communicate your message, the quicker you will build the life of your dreams.

Suggested Reading:

Ursbender, Peter, Secrets of Power Presentations
    The Achievement Group, Toronto, Canada
    (416) 491-6690

FOUR PRINCIPLES OF EFFECTIVE COMMUNICATION

1. ## HAVE A DIRECTION:

    In speaking with a new acquaintance or associate, always remember that the initial purpose is to build rapport. Understand what you expect and what this person expects from this relationship. Be prepared with your questions, know how to get unstuck to minimize time and maximize the interchange.

2. ## PAY ATTENTION TO THE PATTERN OF THE COMMUNICATION:

    Listen with the intent to understand. Realize that most people listen with the intent to reply and therefore rarely do they truly understand. People innately know when you are listening with the intent to understand. This alone makes them feel better about themselves and contributes to creating a good relationship.

3. ## BE FLEXIBLE IN YOUR PATTERN OF QUESTIONING:

    If you notice that the person is uncomfortable, change the direction of the conversation, mimic their body language, and move away if you are seated too close. Sometimes infringing on people's space makes them feel uncomfortable.

4. ## COMMIT TO A SOLUTION:

    If you are a health care practitioner, after your consultation for example, advise the patient that you should continue by performing a complete examination to determine whether or not you are able to provide the answer to their health challenge. In all other professional or business skills, do commit to some form of action step and solution.

    These four skills of communication must be utilized in any and every situation, when speaking with a new acquaintance or associate, an old friend, or a loved one.

THREE INGREDIENTS OF COMMUNICATION

Albert Mehraybiam, a famous researcher from UCLA, discovered that the ingredients of communication included visual, words, and the way the words are said. People are mostly affected by visuals. He reported that 55 percent of the impact of a message was dependent on what the individual saw. The words used accounted for only 7 percent, while the way the words were said (tone of voice, intensity, etc.) accounted for 38 percent of the impact.

To improve your communication skills you therefore need to use visuals (pictures, charts, etc.), speak to the individual in a similar tone and intensity as they are using, and utilize words that are understandable.

If you continuously strive to develop these ingredients, your communication skills will improve and your business will grow. Be sure to remember these ingredients in every conversation in or out of your business life.

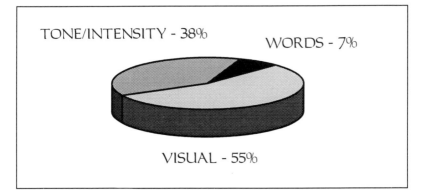

TONE/INTENSITY - 38%

WORDS - 7%

VISUAL - 55%

THREE TECHNIQUES FOR BETTER COMMUNICATION

PACING: (OR BLENDING)

Trying to speak in the tone, speed, and intensity of the person you are conversing with allows better bonding with that individual.

BACKTRACKING:

Utilize something the person says and backtrack with it, for example if you are a doctor and your patient says "I don't feel good", answer with "I understand that you don't feel good, let's see what we might be able to do to help you feel better". In a business situation your customer might say, "I don't like the way this garment fits", you should answer, "I understand you don't like the fit, let's see if we can find one that suits you better."

CLARIFYING:

Repeat what the individual has said and ask them if that is what they meant, or say "I am not understanding exactly what you are telling me, could you clarify this please."

Proper communication skills require practice and coaching. Organizations such as Toastmasters International may be present in your community. Join such a club to develop your skills in public speaking. It is imperative that you get out in your community and share your message with everyone you meet, no matter what type of business you're in.

I have personally developed talks that are not directly related to chiropractic. They do however always contain a chiropractic hope message. Subjects such as "Stress", and "Sports Injuries", have opened so many doors and have accounted for hundreds of new patients attending our clinic for chiropractic health care. The most important public relation tool ever utilized to build and maintain my practice volume has been public speaking.

Prepare a talk that relates to your product, service or idea and practice it with staff, family and friends. Then go out and deliver your message to any size group. Take a leap of faith, you will be thrilled and amazed by the results. This is the most effective and least costly way to advertise your products or services. *Communication is the #1 key to success.*

Without a doubt service excellence is the other key to success in any type of service or business for the future. Strength in these two areas will make the difference between success and mediocrity. If you think of those of your peers who are truly successful in their field, what trait might you say is common to almost all? The answer is usually quite simple: they possess exceptional communication skills. These individuals have developed the ability to establish a rapport with their clients allowing them to build a sense of trust and show enthusiasm for the work they do and the profession that they represent.

Research studies were conducted by the Carnegie Institute of Technology, to determine and evaluate the components of what makes people successful. They found that 15 percent of ones' success is based on technical skills and knowledge, and that 85 percent is derived from your skill in human engineering.

John D. Rockefeller was quoted as saying:

"Communication skills are a commodity that can be purchased in the same way that other skills can be acquired. But, I will pay dearly for that individual who possesses this ability, for it is to be prized above all others."

Success in communication is absolutely necessary in all walks of life. More problems develop in this world as a result of lack of communication than in any other field of human interaction. What successful people do best, is communicate.

Since your relationship with your client is probably the single most important dimension of any business, remember to focus all of your attention on each and every client when they are with you, remembering that they either directly or indirectly purchased the time spent with you. This is nothing more than fulfilling your part of the arrangement and goes a long way towards generating the trust that leads to commitment. Remember to always listen with the intent to understand, otherwise clients will be turned off. It is so important for the client to realize that you care, and therefore show your willingness to understand by listening.

ALWAYS REMEMBER:
THE CLIENT CARES NOT
HOW MUCH YOU KNOW,
UNTIL THEY KNOW
HOW MUCH YOU CARE.

SKILL

'TIS GOD GIVES SKILL,

BUT NOT WITHOUT

MEN'S HANDS:

HE COULD NOT MAKE

ANTONIO STRADIVARIUS

VIOLINS

WITHOUT ANTONIO.

SECTION VI

PERSEVERANCE ALWAYS WINS: COMMITMENT

PERSISTENCE

NOTHING IN THE WORLD CAN
TAKE THE PLACE OF PERSISTENCE

TALENT WILL NOT:
NOTHING IS MORE COMMON
THAN UNSUCCESSFUL PEOPLE
WITH TALENT

GENIUS WILL NOT:
UNREWARDED GENIUS
IS ALMOST A PROVERB

EDUCATION WILL NOT:
THE WORLD IS FULL OF
EDUCATED DERELICTS

PERSISTENCE AND
DETERMINATION ALONE
ARE OMNIPOTENT.

Commitment is the willingness to do whatever it takes to get what you want. A true commitment is a heartfelt promise to yourself from which you will not back down. I urge you to commit to your mission statement and purpose in life. This will give you strength and vision to follow your perfect path to success.

Many people have dreams or good intentions but few are willing to make the commitment necessary for their achievement. No matter how noble your purpose, how clear your vision, or how positive your attitude, what you have envisioned in these exercises for your future will remain a dream unless you are willing to take a stand to be committed.

Kenneth Blanchard, author of <u>The One Minute Manager</u>, states:

> *"There is a difference between interest and commitment. When you are interested in doing something, you do it only when it is convenient. When you are committed to something, you accept no excuses, only results."*

The need for commitment comes from the presence of two phenomena that accompany every human being who has moved forward with purpose and vision in their lives. Any accomplishment of lasting substance appears to occur at the end of some sort of struggle or difficulty. Resistance from anyone to your ideas, can leave you questioning whether or not you should push on, whether or not your vision can be brought to reality.

If you encounter resistance when attempting to achieve your purpose and your goals, realize that all who seek to move beyond mediocrity have faced resistance from family, friends, and other colleagues.

There often appears to be a direct correlation between the power of an idea and the actual resistance you must face.

Albert Einstein stated:

"Great spirits have always encountered violent opposition from mediocre minds."

Commitment is the ending of resistance. It is the promise to yourself to press on, to get up one more time than you fall. If you truly believe in your purpose and your vision, believing that its achievement is worth the effort, realize that there may be tradeoffs along the way. Commitment is the mental resolve to never give up. Determined action is the evidence of that resolve. Success requires both mental and physical effort.

If this sounds like hard work, consider the alternatives, the life of the uncommitted. For those people, there is no reason to rise in the morning or to go to bed at night. Each day comes after the next and survival appears to be the key issue.

Life is meant to be lived one moment at a time. You should enjoy the journey every moment of every single day. Since life occurs for each of us to grow and contribute, be committed to follow your path that will lead to fulfillment of your mission. When truly committed, you will attract people, events and situations into your life, that you may not have thought possible.

This will not be a coincidence, but merely a reflection of your commitment to achieve, to help others, to be the total person that you can be. Integrity, purpose and commitment are the three ingredients that will allow you to *steer your ship called life*.

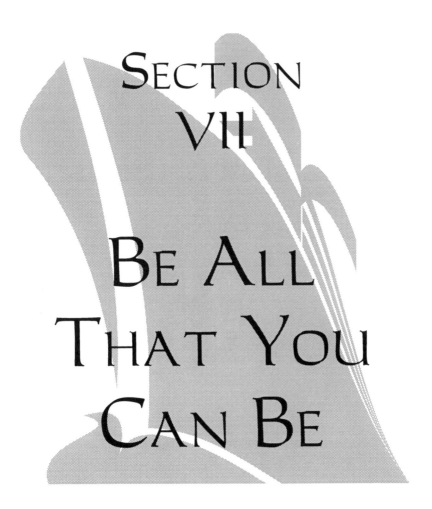

SECTION VII

BE ALL THAT YOU CAN BE

"LIFE IS A DARING ADVENTURE OR NOTHING."

Helen Keller

Every morning upon awakening, take a moment to give thanks for the blessings that will come your way as you begin another day of life. Be willing to utilize your talents to help others, be willing to give others a push whenever necessary.

Envision your life as a masterpiece and yourself as the artist holding the brush. Apply the colours, create the bright visions, be all that you can be. You have been given great gifts – share them.

BE

ALL THAT

YOU CAN BE.

You are an instrument with every tool at your side to guide yourself and others to truly experience the miracle of life. There is real magic in the human being and you possess what is necessary to share this message and this wealth. You are here to enjoy life to the fullest, to love and to serve. Be thankful for the opportunity to serve others; let the beauty of what you love, be what you do.

Remember that you make a living by what you get, but more importantly, make a life by what you give. Be willing to share your talent and your love for people and life with everyone you meet. Your work will be love made visible. Give for the sake of giving, love for the sake of loving, live for the sake of living.

Every night upon retiring, remember to give thanks and count the enormous blessings that have been bestowed upon you and you will become the Captain, STEERING YOUR SHIP CALLED LIFE.

CONCLUSION

A long time ago I learned that a genius is simply one that listens to the spirit, wisdom and light of his/her soul and obeys. They obey that inner calling, they follow without question. That has been my motivation. If you are interested in upgrading your thinking, you must feed your mind properly.

Follow my recipe:

1. *Read something inspirational daily*

2. *Listen to positive message cassette tapes daily.*

3. *Think of what you want to be, do or have – you become what you think of most.*

4. *Associate with positive, upbeat, happy and healthy people.*

5. *Laugh, sing and talk about the good things in life – always in positive terms.*

6. *Have fun – and remember to say thank you.*

In closing, I share these special poems and quotations, which will bring insight to your mind, warmth to your heart and gratitude to your soul.

The spirit in me salutes the spirit in you.

Love and affection,

Gilles

IF WE CAN DREAM IT, WE CAN MAKE IT COME TRUE.

"THE GREATEST GIFT
ONE PERSON CAN GIVE
TO ANOTHER IS A DEEPER
UNDERSTANDING OF LIFE
AND THE ABILITY TO LOVE
AND BELIEVE IN ONESELF."

Tammy J. Noble

THE SPIRITUAL MINUTE

BE AWARE OF YOUR THOUGHTS ...
  THEY BECOME WORDS

BE AWARE OF YOUR WORDS ...
  THEY BECOME ACTIONS

BE AWARE OF YOUR ACTIONS ...
  THEY BECOME HABITS

BE AWARE OF YOUR HABITS ...
  THEY BECOME YOUR CHARACTER

BE AWARE OF YOUR CHARACTER ...
  IT IS YOUR DESTINY

Frank Outlaw

"EVERY GOOD THOUGHT

YOU THINK

IS CONTRIBUTING

ITS SHARE TO THE

ULTIMATE RESULT

OF YOUR LIFE."

Grenville Kleiser

"IF A MAN DOES NOT KNOW WHAT PORT HE IS STEERING FOR, NO WIND WILL BE FAVOURABLE TO HIM."

Seneca

WITHOUT

100%

THERE IS NO

COMMITMENT.

LEARNING HAS NOT TAKEN PLACE UNTIL BEHAVIOUR HAS CHANGED.

Pike's Fourth Law

"DIGNITY

DOES NOT CONSIST

IN POSSESSING HONORS,

BUT IN DESERVING THEM."

Aristotle

"All that is

comes from the mind;

it is based on the mind,

it is fashioned

by the mind."

The Pali Cannon
500 - 250 B.C.

LIFE IS NOT FOR WHINING OR WORRYING ...

LIFE

IS FOR

LAUGHING

LOVING

AND

LIVING

THE HIGHEST PRIVILEGE

ON EARTH

IS TO BE ABLE TO

LOSE YOURSELF

IN SERVICE TO

THE HUMAN RACE.

TAKE TIME FOR TEN THINGS

TAKE TIME TO WORK, IT IS THE PRICE OF SUCCESS.

TAKE TIME TO THINK, IT IS THE SOURCE OF POWER.

TAKE TIME TO PLAY, IT IS THE SECRET OF YOUTH.

TAKE TIME TO READ, IT IS THE FOUNTAIN OF KNOWLEDGE.

TAKE TIME TO WORSHIP, IT IS THE HIGHWAY OF REVERENCE
THAT WASHES THE DUST OF EARTH FROM OUR EYES.

TAKE TIME TO HELP AND ENJOY FRIENDS, IT IS THE SOURCE
OF HAPPINESS.

TAKE TIME TO LOVE, IT IS THE ONE SACRAMENT OF LIFE.

TAKE TIME TO DREAM, IT HITCHES THE SOUL TO THE STARS.

TAKE TIME TO LAUGH, IT IS THE SINGING THAT HELPS
WITH LIFE'S LOAD'S.

TAKE TIME TO PLAN, IT IS THE SECRET OF BEING ABLE
TO TAKE TIME FOR THE FIRST NINE THINGS.

LET THERE BE

PEACE ON EARTH

AND LET IT BEGIN

WITH ME.

MAY YOU ALWAYS BE INSPIRED ...

TO STAND TALL IN THE SUNLIGHT.

TO SEEK OUT THE BRIGHT FACE OF BEAUTY.

TO REACH FOR THE DREAM, THE STAR.

TO SEE THE WORLD THROUGH THE EYES
OF TENDERNESS.

TO SPEAK THE QUIET WORD OF COMFORTING.

TO LOOK UP THE MOUNTAIN
AND NOT BE AFRAID TO CLIMB.

TO BE AWARE OF THE NEEDS OF OTHERS.

TO BELIEVE IN THE WONDER OF LIFE,

THE MIRACLE OF CREATION,

THE RAPTURE OF LOVE,

THE BEAUTY OF THE UNIVERSE,

THE DIGNITY OF THE HUMAN BEING.

H. Marshall